Etta Kaner

Do NOT Eat Like a Tiger Shark!

Wacky Ways Animals Slurp, Chomp and Gulp

illustrated by
Heather Wilson

ORCA BOOK PUBLISHERS

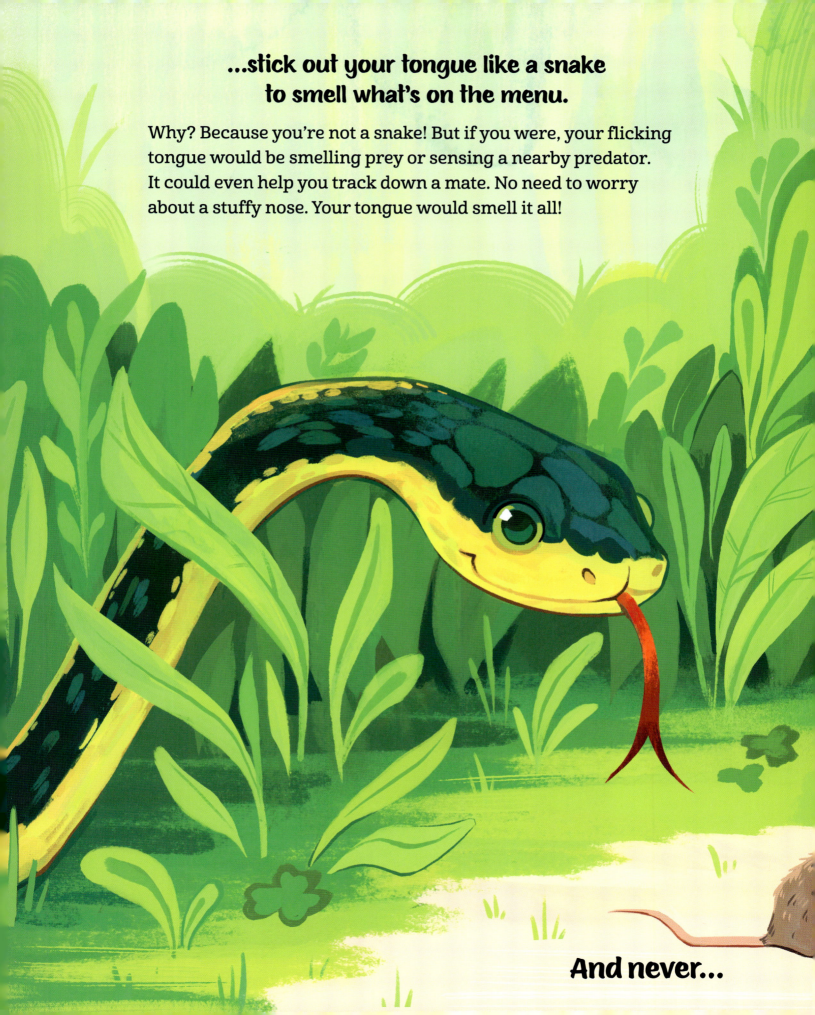

...stick out your tongue like a snake to smell what's on the menu.

Why? Because you're not a snake! But if you were, your flicking tongue would be smelling prey or sensing a nearby predator. It could even help you track down a mate. No need to worry about a stuffy nose. Your tongue would smell it all!

And never...

No, flamingos don't stand on their heads to eat. That would be ridiculous. A flamingo just turns its *head* and *bill* upside down. Why? A flamingo's bill needs to scoop up algae, shrimp and insects from lake water. But only the *upper* half of its bill can open and close. So the bird just flips its head around so that the moving part of the bill is at the bottom. Problem solved!

And do not...

Favorite activity for Tasmanian devils? Tearing into rotting dead animals (carrion) with their strong jaws. Mmm...dead meat! As if that's not bad enough, a Tasmanian devil likes to fall asleep inside the carrion so that it can continue eating when it wakes up. Eww!

And please don't...

...drink your milk with your nose, elephant-style.

Oops! Sorry about that. Elephants do *not* drink with their trunks. An elephant uses its trunk like a powerful vacuum cleaner to suck up water (not milk). Its trunk can hold about 10.5 quarts (10 liters) of water at one time. That's the same as five large soda bottles! Whenever an elephant is thirsty—SQUIRT! Water goes from the trunk into its mouth.

And never ever...

...swallow your food whole like an Amazon horned frog.

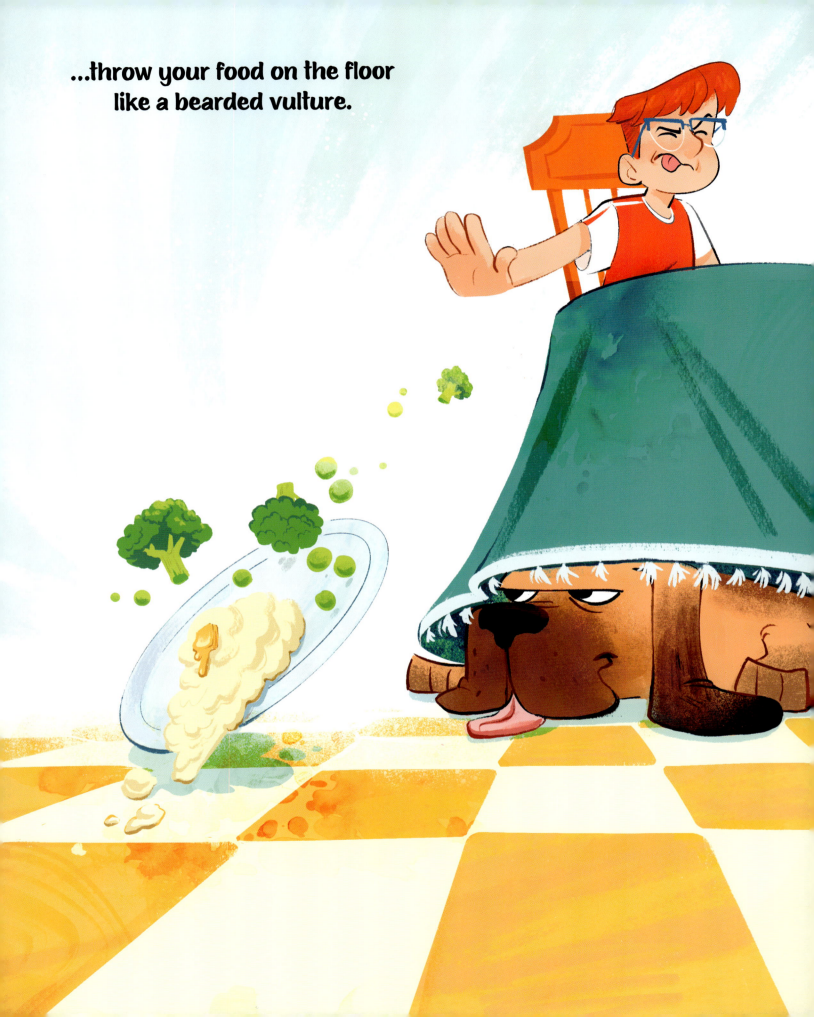
...throw your food on the floor like a bearded vulture.

Does this bird throw temper tantrums? Nope. It's just trying to crack open the large bone of a dead animal and get at the yummy marrow inside. So how does it do this? It grabs the bone in its feet, flies up high and drops it onto rocks below! Dinnertime!

And you shouldn't...

...hide your food around the house like a black-capped chickadee.

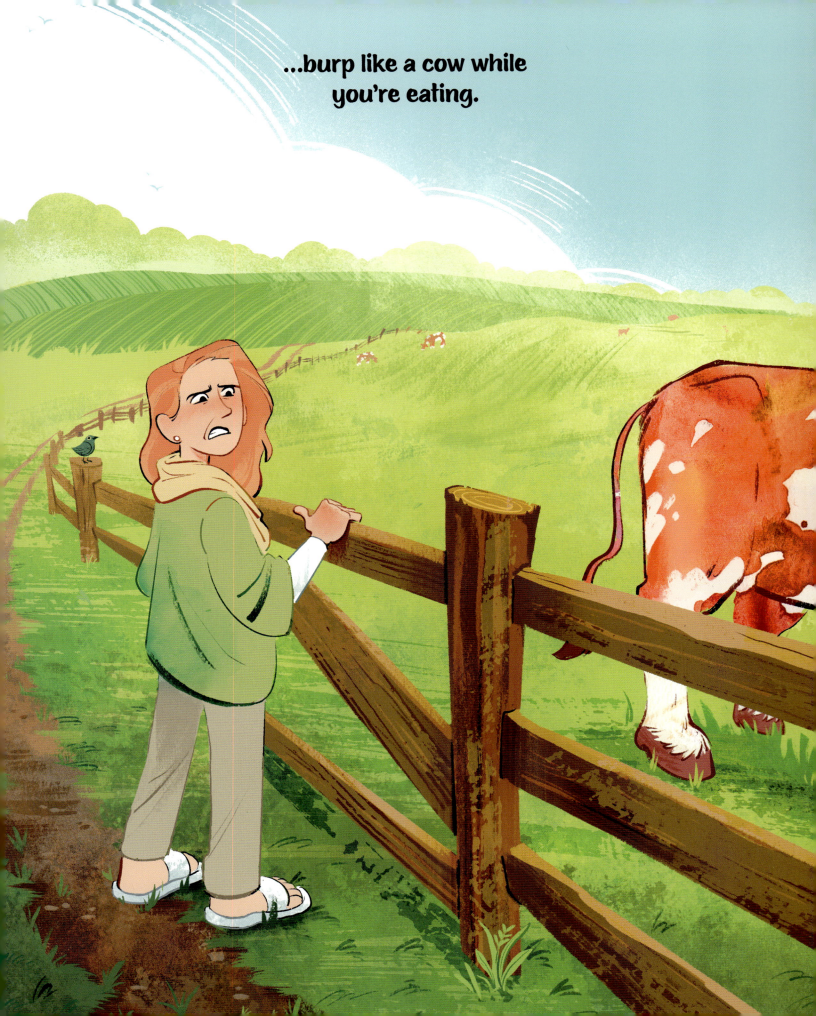

It *is* gross. But cows can't help burping. That's the way their stomachs work. The grass they eat makes gas inside their stomachs. When the gases build up, it really hurts. So how does a cow get rid of the gas?

BURP!

And ALWAYS...

...say "thank you" before leaving the table.
Because you are a person, and that's what people do!

More Fascinating Facts

Snakes
Wonder why a snake's tongue is forked? The forks allow the snake to know which direction a scent is coming from—the left or the right.

Butterflies
Butterflies also have taste buds on the knobs of their antennae. They pick up scents from the air, which tell the butterflies where to find food or a mate.

Dogs
Dogs also use their tongues to eat, groom their fur, explore their world and cool down when they're too hot.

Flamingos
A flamingo's mouth acts like a sieve. The bird fills its bill with water, algae, shrimp and insects. The tongue pushes the water out through tiny comb-like ridges along the edges of the bill. The food stays inside.

Tasmanian devils
If it's *really* hungry, a Tasmanian devil can eat up to 40 percent of its body weight in half an hour. That's like you eating about 60 apples in one meal!

Elephants
An elephant's trunk is all muscle. Actually, more than 40,000 muscles! To eat, an elephant uses its trunk to crush leaves, fruit and roots into a solid clump that can be picked up easily.

Amazon horned frogs

To catch prey, this sneaky frog hides in leaf litter, where its colors blend right in. Passing prey never suspect that there's a frog nearby, ready to pounce on it for lunch.

Bearded vultures

Once a bearded vulture has enjoyed the marrow inside a bone, it swallows the bone. Doesn't it get a stomach ache? No! Its stomach acids break down bones quickly.

Guenons

The Allen's swamp monkey is a type of guenon that goes fishing. It places leaves or grass on the water's surface. When a fish hides underneath, the monkey grabs it.

Tiger sharks

Tiger sharks are really aggressive. Most animals don't eat their own species, but tiger sharks do! Adults will eat juveniles (young tiger sharks).

Black-capped chickadees

To make sure it will have enough food during the winter, the black-capped chickadee hides seeds. About one thousand of them. Each in its own place. And it remembers where it hid every one!

Cows

Cow burps aren't just smelly. They produce methane, a gas that contributes to global warming. Scientists hope that getting cows to eat garlic, charcoal or seaweed will reduce the methane in their burps.

For Yael and Zion, with love.
—E.K.

**Mom and Dad—
thank you for the endless support and
tolerating my weird antics.**
—H.W.

Text copyright © Etta Kaner 2024
Illustrations copyright © Heather Wilson 2024

Published in Canada and the United States in 2024 by Orca Book Publishers.
orcabook.com

All rights are reserved, including those for text and data mining, AI training and similar technologies. No part of this publication may be reproduced or transmitted in any form or by any means, electronic or mechanical, including photocopying, recording or by any information storage and retrieval system now known or to be invented, without permission in writing from the publisher. The publisher expressly prohibits the use of this work in connection with the development of any software program, including, without limitation, training a machine learning or generative artificial intelligence (AI) system.

Library and Archives Canada Cataloguing in Publication

Title: Do NOT eat like a tiger shark! : wacky ways animals slurp, chomp and gulp / Etta Kaner ; illustrated by Heather Wilson.
Names: Kaner, Etta, author. | Wilson, Heather (Illustrator), illustrator.
Identifiers: Canadiana (print) 20230542816 | Canadiana (ebook) 20230542824 |
ISBN 9781459838130 (hardcover) | ISBN 9781459838147 (PDF) | ISBN 9781459838154 (EPUB)
Subjects: LCSH: Animals—Food—Juvenile literature. | LCSH: Animals—Food—Humor—Juvenile literature. |
LCSH: Animal behavior—Juvenile literature. | LCSH: Animal behavior—Humor—Juvenile literature. |
LCGFT: Instructional and educational works. | LCGFT: Illustrated works. | LCGFT: Humor.
Classification: LCC QL756.5 .K36 2024 | DDC j591.5/3—dc23

Library of Congress Control Number: 2023946362

Summary: This humorous illustrated nonfiction picture book looks at the unusual ways that animals eat and drink.

Orca Book Publishers is committed to reducing the consumption of nonrenewable resources in the production of our books.
We make every effort to use materials that support a sustainable future.

Orca Book Publishers gratefully acknowledges the support for its publishing programs provided by the following agencies: the Government of Canada, the Canada Council for the Arts and the Province of British Columbia through the BC Arts Council and the Book Publishing Tax Credit.

The author and publisher have made every effort to ensure that the information in this book was correct at the time of publication. The author and publisher do not assume any liability for any loss, damage, or disruption caused by errors or omissions. Every effort has been made to trace copyright holders and to obtain their permission for the use of copyrighted material. The publisher apologizes for any errors or omissions and would be grateful if notified of any corrections that should be incorporated in future reprints or editions of this book.

Artwork created digitally in Procreate with additional hand-painted texture details.

Cover and interior artwork by Heather Wilson
Design by Rachel Page and Heather Wilson
Edited by Kirstie Hudson

Printed and bound in South Korea.

27 26 25 24 • 1 2 3 4

Etta Kaner is an award-winning, internationally known author whose nonfiction books for children have been translated into many languages. A former teacher, she is passionate about science books for young readers. When she's not writing, Etta loves trying out new recipes at her home in Toronto.

Heather Wilson is a Canadian illustrator and animation designer. She is a graduate of Sheridan College's illustration program and recipient of the Brenda Clark Visual Narrative Award. Heather grew up on a southern Ontario farm, among cornstalks and strawberry fields. She now resides in Oakville, overlooking Lake Ontario.